Pandas

Have

Cubs

by Emily J. Dolbear and E. Russell Primm

Animals and Their Young

Content Advisers: Terrence E. Young Jr., M.Ed., M.L.S.
Jefferson Parish (La.) Public Schools, and Janann Jenner, Ph. D.

Reading Adviser: Dr. Linda D. Labbo,
Department of Reading Education, College of Education,
The University of Georgia

COMPASS POINT BOOKS

Minneapolis, Minnesota

Compass Point Books
3109 West 50th Street, #115
Minneapolis, MN 55410

Visit Compass Point Books on the Internet at *www.compasspointbooks.com* or e-mail your request to
custserv@compasspointbooks.com

Photographs ©: Keren Su/FPG International, cover; Tom & Pat Leeson, 4, 16, 18; Heather Angel, 6, 20; Keren
Su/China Span, 8, 10, 12; Lynn Stone, 14.

Editors: E. Russell Primm and Emily J. Dolbear
Photo Researcher: Svetlana Zhurkina
Photo Selector: Linda S. Koutris
Designer: Bradfordesign, Inc.

Library of Congress Cataloging-in-Publication Data

Dolbear, Emily J.
    Pandas have cubs / by Emily J. Dolbear and E. Russell Primm III.
      p. cm. — (Animals and their young)
    Includes bibliographical references (p.   ).
    ISBN 0-7565-0062-1 (hardcover)
    ISBN 0-7565-1244-1 (paperback)
      1. Giant panda—Infancy—Juvenile literature. [1. Giant panda. 2. Pandas. 3. Animals—Infancy.] I. Primm, E.
Russell, 1958– . II. Title. III. Series.
QL737.C214 D66 2001
599.789—dc21
                                              00-011684

Table of Contents

What Are Cubs?

Baby pandas are called **cubs**. There are no special names for mother and father pandas. They live only in China.

Pandas are also called giant pandas. Once, people thought that giant pandas were related to red pandas. Red pandas are smaller animals with red fur. Now, scientists know that red pandas are really raccoons. They also know that giant pandas are really bears.

These panda cubs are nearly full grown.

What Happens before Cubs Are Born?

In late summer, the mother panda looks for a place to give birth. She searches for a hollow tree or a small rocky spot. She needs a safe place for her baby cub.

A mother panda carries her baby inside her body for 97 to 165 days. A mother panda gives birth once every one to three years. She has one or two cubs. Sometimes, she has three cubs at a time. Usually only one cub lives.

◀ A mother panda looks for a safe place to give birth to her cub.

What Happens after Cubs Are Born?

A newborn cub weighs 3 to 5 ounces (85 to 142 grams). It is about the size of a **chipmunk**.

A newborn panda is helpless. It depends on its mother for everything. The mother feeds the cub. The cub cries when it is hungry like a human baby. The mother panda keeps it warm and safe. She also cleans the cub.

◄ A newborn panda rests on a towel.

How Do Cubs Feed?

When the cub is born, the mother panda quickly pulls it to her chest. She cuddles the cub. Almost at once, the cub **nurses**, or drinks its mother's milk. She holds her cub the way a human mother holds her baby. The cub may nurse as often as twelve times a day.

What Does a Cub Look Like?

A newborn panda cub does not look much like its parents. It has pink skin and short, white fur. Its fur is so thin that its pink skin shows through. Soon the cub's skin will turn gray in the places where black fur will grow. When it is one month old, the cub looks much like its parents.

What Colors Are Cubs?

A panda cub has black patches on its white coat. These patches are on its ears, around its eyes, and across its shoulders. It has black legs too. The panda's fur is thick and woolly. Oily fur helps keep the panda cub dry and warm.

People have seen rare brown and white pandas in the wild. The pandas' color helps them blend into their surroundings. It helps hide them from enemies, such as snow leopards and wild dogs.

◄ Pandas have black patches of fur on their ears and shoulders and around their eyes.

What Do Young Cubs Do and Eat?

Panda cubs love to play. When the cubs are bigger, the mother may toss her cub between her front paws. The cub seems to like this. The mother also rolls around with her baby.

When they are five or six months old, cubs begin eating solid food. First, they eat only the tender leaves of the **bamboo** plant. When the cubs are about one year old, their adult teeth come in. Then they eat bamboo stems and wood as well as leaves.

◄ Pandas spend most of the day eating bamboo.

What Happens As a Cub Grows Older?

When it is about three months old, a panda cub moves farther away from its mother. When a cub is about one year old, it weighs 75 to 100 pounds (34 to 45 kilograms).

A mother panda teaches her cubs how to find and eat bamboo. Panda cubs eat between 20 and 40 pounds (9 to 18 kilograms) of bamboo a day. It takes a panda ten to sixteen hours every day to eat this much food.

◀ Two panda cubs play with each other.

When Is a Cub Grown Up?

When it is about eighteen months old, a panda cub is full grown. It is about the same size as an American black bear. An adult male panda weighs between 176 to 350 pounds (80 to 160 kilograms). Females are smaller.

Only about 1,000 pandas live in the wild today. Giant pandas in the wild live to be between fifteen and twenty-five years old. The oldest panda in a zoo lived to be thirty-seven!

There aren't many pandas left in the wild.

Glossary

bamboo—a grass with hard, hollow stems that grows in warm places

chipmunk—a ground squirrel

cubs—baby pandas

nurse—to drink milk produced by the mother

Did You Know?

- The Chinese name for a panda is *xiongmao*. It means "great bear cat."

- Chinese emperors kept pandas as pets.

- The ancient Chinese believed that pandas had special powers to warn of disaster and evil spirits.

- Adult pandas are 4 to 6 feet (122 to 183 centimeters) long.

- Female pandas can have cubs when they are four to ten years old.

Want to Know More?

At the Library

Fitzsimons, Cecilia, and Jo Moore (illustrator). *Giant Pandas Eat All Day Long*. Brookfield, Conn.: Millbrook Press, 2000.

Fowler, Allan. *Giant Pandas: Gifts from China*. Chicago: Children's Press, 1995.

Tracqui, Valerie. *The Panda: Wild about Bamboo*. Cambridge, Mass.: Charlesbridge Publishing, 1999.

On the Web

Panda Cam

http://www.sandiegozoo.org/special/pandas/pandacam/index.html

For live video of panda Bai Yun and her cub, Hua Mei, at the San Diego Zoo

SchoolWorld Internet Panda Project

http://www.schoolworld.asn.au/species/panda.html

For information about giant pandas and their life cycles

Through the Mail

World Wildlife Fund for Nature

1250 24th Street, N.W.

Washington, DC 20037-1175

To get information about this group's work to save pandas and other animals in danger

On the Road

San Diego Zoo

2920 Zoo Drive

San Diego, CA 92103

619/234-3153

To visit Bai Yun and her cub, Hua Mei, at this world-famous zoo

Index

About the Authors

Emily J. Dolbear has been an editor for Franklin Watts, Children's Press, and The Ecco Press. She now works as a freelance writer and editor. She lives in Chicago with her husband and son.

E. Russell Primm has worked as an editor for more than twenty years. He has been editorial director for Ferguson Publishing Company and for Children's Press and Franklin Watts. He now heads Editorial Directions, a book-producing and consulting company. He lives in Chicago.